Hamlyn all-colour cookbooks

Family
Cooking

Marguerite Patten

Hamlyn
London · New York · Sydney · Toronto

Published by
The Hamlyn Publishing Group Limited
London · New York · Sydney · Toronto
Hamlyn House, Feltham, Middlesex, England
© Copyright The Hamlyn Publishing Group Limited 1973
ISBN 0 600 30198 2
Printed in England by Sir Joseph Causton and Sons Limited
Line drawings by John Scott Martin

Contents

Useful facts and figures

Note on metrication

In this book quantities are given in both Imperial and metric measures. Exact conversion from Imperial to metric does not always give very convenient working quantities so for greater convenience and ease of working we have taken an equivalent of 25 grammes/millilitres to the ounce/fluid ounce. 1 oz. is exactly 28·35 g. and $\frac{1}{4}$ pint (5 fl. oz.) is 142 ml., so you will see that by using the unit of 25 you will get a slightly smaller result than the Imperial measures would give.

Occasionally, for example in a basic recipe such as a Victoria sandwich made with 4 oz. flour, butter and sugar and 2 eggs, we have rounded the conversion up to give a more generous result. For larger amounts where the exact conversion is not critical, for instance in soups or stews, we have used kilogrammes and fractions (1 kg. equals 2·2 lb.) and litres and fractions (1 litre equals 1·76 pints). All recipes have been individually converted so that each recipe preserves the correct proportions.

Oven temperatures

The following chart gives the Celsius (Centigrade) equivalents recommended by the Electricity Council.

Description	Fahrenheit	Celsius	Gas Mark
Very cool	225	110	$\frac{1}{4}$
	250	130	$\frac{1}{2}$
Cool	275	140	1
	300	150	2
Moderate	325	170	3
	350	180	4
Moderately hot	375	190	5
	400	200	6
Hot	425	220	7
	450	230	8
Very hot	475	240	9

Introduction

Sometimes it is difficult to ring the changes when you are cooking for the family. Trying to find a dish to suit the budget and your husband and children can often lead to a lack of variety in the menus. I hope that this all-colour recipe book will give you instant inspiration, as there is a colour picture which will help you with the presentation and garnishing of each finished dish.

I have included a great variety of dishes using inexpensive fish, cheaper cuts of meat and, of course, chicken. There are also some more exotic dishes for special occasions.

If you are short of time, as most of us are, try planning ahead to enable you to use the oven for two or three dishes at the same time. This can save you time another day if you are able to store a casserole and perhaps a pudding in the refrigerator.

Working wives should become familiar with the automatic oven as it can save chaos when you arrive home in the evening.

In order to have the maximum success with the recipes in this book, read them through quickly before starting to assemble the ingredients. In this way you will ensure that you have sufficient time to cook the dish, and that you have all the ingredients for the recipe, before starting the preparation.

These recipes are well tried and tested favourites and I hope that they will become popular with your family.

Paella

Cooking time: 25–30 minutes
Preparation time: 15 minutes
Main cooking utensil: frying pan
Serves: 4

Imperial	Metric
2 tablespoons oil	2 tablespoons oil
1 chopped onion	1 chopped onion
3 skinned tomatoes	3 skinned tomatoes
3–4 oz. long-grain rice	75–100 g. long-grain rice
pinch saffron powder	pinch saffron powder
1 pint chicken stock	550 ml. chicken stock
seasoning	seasoning
1 small green pepper	1 small green pepper
¾–1 lb. white fish, preferably skate or other firm-textured fish	300–400 g. white fish, preferably skate or other firm-textured fish
4–5 oz. prawns	100–125 g. prawns
To garnish:	*To garnish:*
few prawns in their shells	few prawns in their shells
chopped parsley	chopped parsley

1. Heat the oil in a large frying pan; fry the finely chopped onion and large pieces of tomato for a few minutes.
2. Add the rice, turn in the oil, then add the saffron blended with the chicken stock. Season well.
3. Simmer gently for 5–10 minutes.
4. Add the chopped green pepper, removing seeds and core, and the pieces of fish.
5. Cook until both fish and rice are soft.
6. Add the prawns, heat for a few minutes only.
7. Garnish with prawns and parsley. Serve with salad.

Variation
A more authentic paella is made by adding 1–2 crushed cloves of garlic, tiny pieces of uncooked chicken in place of white fish, and mussels and lobster as well as prawns.

Salmon pie

Cooking time: 40 minutes
Preparation time: 30 minutes
Main cooking utensils: saucepans, flat baking tray or sheet
Oven temperature: hot (425–450°F., 220–230°C., Gas Mark 7–8)
    then moderately hot (400°F., 200°C., Gas Mark 6)
Oven position: centre
Serves: 4–6

Imperial	Metric
12 oz. puff pastry	300 g. puff pastry
1 can quick-cooking rice	1 can quick-cooking rice
1 small onion	1 small onion
$\frac{1}{2}$ oz. butter	15 g. butter
3 tablespoons cream or white sauce	3 tablespoons cream or white sauce
1 tablespoon chopped parsley	1 tablespoon chopped parsley
12-oz. can salmon	300-g. can salmon
2 hard-boiled eggs	2 hard-boiled eggs
seasoning	seasoning
little butter (about $\frac{1}{2}$ oz.)	little butter (about 15 g.)
To garnish:	*To garnish:*
parsley	parsley
lemon	lemon

1. If using frozen puff pastry allow it to defrost enough to roll out.

2. Cook the rice as directed, then drain and dry.

3. Chop the onion and cook in the hot butter, then add the cream, parsley, flaked salmon, and rice.

4. Roll out the pastry to an oblong about 15 inches by 12 inches (35 by 30 cm.). Put the salmon mixture on this, then cover with the sliced hard-boiled eggs, seasoning and tiny pieces of butter.

5. Damp the edges of the pastry and fold to cover the filling.

6. Secure the ends of the pastry; snip the top pastry to allow steam to escape.

7. Bake for time and at temperature given, reducing the heat after about 20 minutes. Garnish with parsley and lemon slices.

Note: This pie is excellent for taking on a picnic as it can be wrapped in foil and carried safely.

Variation

Use 3 oz. (75 g.) long-grain rice instead of the canned rice. Add a little lemon juice to flavour the filling.

Macaroni fish pie

Cooking time: 15–25 minutes
Preparation time: 10–12 minutes
Main cooking utensils: 2 saucepans, ovenproof dish
Serves: 4

Imperial	Metric
3 oz. macaroni	75 g. macaroni
water	water
salt	salt
1 lb. white fish	400 g. white fish
Cheese sauce:	*Cheese sauce:*
1 oz. butter or margarine	25 g. butter or margarine
1 oz. flour	25 g. flour
½ pint milk	250 ml. milk
seasoning	seasoning
pinch dry mustard	pinch dry mustard
3 oz. grated Cheddar cheese	75 g. grated Cheddar cheese

1. If using long macaroni, break it into small pieces. Cook in a scant 2 pints (1 litre) boiling salted water until tender. If using elbow-length macaroni, cook as directed on the packet.
2. Meanwhile simmer fish in a little salted water until tender but not too soft.
3. Lift fish out and break into fairly big flakes.
4. Heat butter or margarine in a pan, stir in flour, cook 'roux' for 2–3 minutes over a low heat. Remove from the heat, gradually add the milk and seasoning.
5. Bring to the boil, cook until thickened, then add grated cheese; do not boil after this.
6. Put drained macaroni and fish into a hot dish, top with cheese sauce.
7. Put for 2–3 minutes under a hot grill until the top is bubbly. Serve with a green vegetable – e.g., spinach – or a green salad. Potatoes are not necessary.

Variation
Macaroni fish pie au gratin: Top with breadcrumbs and grated cheese before browning.

Baked stuffed fillets of haddock

Cooking time: 2½ hours
Preparation time: 20 minutes plus overnight soaking for beans
Main cooking utensils: saucepan, baking dish, foil
Oven temperature: moderate (350°F., 180°C., Gas Mark 4)
Oven position: centre
Serves: 4–6

Imperial	Metric
8 oz. butter beans	200 g. butter beans
salt	salt
bay leaf	bay leaf
Stuffing:	*Stuffing:*
1 oz. chopped onion	25 g. chopped onion
2 oz. butter	50 g. butter
2 oz. shelled walnuts, coarsely chopped	50 g. shelled walnuts, coarsely chopped
2 sprigs rosemary	2 sprigs rosemary
$\frac{1}{2}$ teaspoon dried fennel	$\frac{1}{2}$–1 teaspoon dried fennel
3 oz. brown breadcrumbs	75 g. brown breadcrumbs
seasoning	seasoning
1 egg yolk	1 egg yolk
2 fresh haddock fillets (each 8–10 oz.)	2 fresh haddock fillets (each 200–250 g.)
To garnish:	*To garnish:*
6 small tomatoes	6 small tomatoes
chopped parsley	chopped parsley
lemon slices	lemon slices

1. Soak beans overnight in enough water to cover.
2. Cook gently for 2 hours with salt and bay leaf.
3. Meanwhile chop the onion, cook with 1 oz. (25 g.) butter until soft.
4. Put in the walnuts, brown slightly.
5. Add the finely chopped rosemary and fennel to breadcrumbs.
6. Stir into the onion, season and bind with the egg.
7. Cover one fillet with the stuffing then top with the second fillet. Wrap in buttered foil, put into a dish and bake for 25 minutes. Add the tomatoes towards the end of cooking time.
8. Lift the fish out of the dish, put the drained beans in the dish, and put back the fish on top.
9. Brown remaining butter and pour over fish. Garnish with parsley and lemon slices and serve hot.

Variation
Use chives and parsley instead of rosemary and fennel.

Cutlets espagnole

Cooking time: 10 minutes
Preparation time: 10–15 minutes
Main cooking utensil: grill pan
Serves: 3

Imperial	Metric
3 large cod cutlets	3 large cod cutlets
juice of 1 lemon	juice of 1 lemon
seasoning	seasoning
$\frac{1}{2}$ oz. melted butter	15 g. melted butter
6 oz. grated cheese	150 g. grated cheese
1 tablespoon mixed herbs	1 tablespoon mixed herbs
1 small finely chopped onion	1 small finely chopped onion
1 oz. butter	25 g. butter
1 large tomato	1 large tomato
To garnish:	*To garnish:*
parsley	parsley
lemon slices	lemon slices

1. Wash the cutlets and dry thoroughly.
2. Squeeze lemon juice on each cutlet and season well; brush with melted butter.
3. Grill on underside for 3—5 minutes.
4. Mix grated cheese, herbs and chopped onion together. Add a little lemon juice.
5. Divide mixture into three portions and form each portion into a firm ball.
6. Place a portion of cheese mixture on each of the cutlets, add a knob of butter on each cutlet.
7. Place under a hot grill and cook for about 4—5 minutes, or until cutlets are cooked through, adding sliced tomato topped with butter towards the end of cooking time. Dish up immediately after cooking as cheese mixture may toughen. Garnish with parsley and tomato, and slices of lemon.

Note: The cheese must be formed into a ball otherwise it will have melted long before the fish is cooked.

Variation
Use haddock or turbot cutlets.

Cod portugaise

Cooking time: 20—25 minutes
Preparation time: 15 minutes
Main cooking utensils: frying pan, saucepan
Serves: 4

Imperial	**Metric**
Portuguese sauce:	*Portuguese sauce:*
1 tablespoon oil	1 tablespoon oil
1 medium onion	1 medium onion
¼ green pepper	¼ green pepper
4 medium tomatoes	4 medium tomatoes
1 lb. cod fillets	400 g. cod fillets
1 tablespoon flour	1 tablespoon flour
seasoning	seasoning
1–2 tablespoons oil	1–2 tablespoons oil
2 oz. butter	50 g. butter
⅓ pint white wine	175 ml. white wine
about 12 stuffed olives	about 12 stuffed olives

1. Heat oil in a saucepan and cook finely chopped onion till tender, but not brown.

2. Remove seeds from the green pepper, slice the flesh and add to onion. Cook lightly for a few minutes.

3. Skin tomatoes, quarter and remove pips. Tip into the onion mixture, keep warm.

4. Skin fillets and cut into four pieces, coat in seasoned flour.

5. Heat oil in a large frying pan, add butter for flavour. When fat is hot, lay fish in the pan and let it cook briskly but not violently.

6. When one side is browned, turn and cook other side of each piece.

7. Add wine and olives to tomato mixture and heat.

8. Pour a little sauce into a serving dish, top with fish and serve the rest of the sauce separately. Accompany by green vegetables, plain boiled potatoes.

Variation
Turbot and halibut are both good cooked in this way.

Smoked haddock kedgeree

Cooking time: 30 minutes
Preparation time: 15 minutes
Main cooking utensils: 2 saucepans
Serves: 4–6

Imperial	Metric
1 medium-sized smoked haddock	1 medium-sized smoked haddock
water	water
3 oz. long-grain rice	75 g. long-grain rice
seasoning	seasoning
bay leaf	bay leaf
slice lemon	slice lemon
2 oz. butter	50 g. butter
1 small onion	1 small onion
To garnish:	*To garnish:*
1–2 hard-boiled eggs	1–2 hard-boiled eggs
parsley	parsley
paprika pepper	paprika pepper

1. Cut the haddock into neat pieces and put into a pan with cold water, bring just to the boil, then remove the pan from the heat – this method of poaching the fish prevents over-cooking.

2. Put the rice into the second pan with $\frac{1}{4}$ pint (125 ml.) water only; add seasoning, the bay leaf and lemon.

3. Bring the water to the boil, stir briskly, cover the pan tightly, then lower the heat and cook slowly for approximately 15 minutes – by this time the water will have been absorbed and the rice will be tender.

4. Heat the butter and fry the finely chopped onion until tender, then add the fish and the rice and heat together.

5. Pile on to a hot dish and top with halved eggs, sprigs of parsley and paprika pepper. Serve with crisp toast.

Variations

Omit the onion, and add a little cream. Omit the onion and fry a little chopped bacon with the butter.

Salmon layer betty

Cooking time: 25 minutes
Preparation time: 10 minutes
Main cooking utensils: frying pan, 1½-pint (¾-litre) ovenproof dish
Oven temperature: moderately hot (375–400°F., 190–200°C., Gas
  Mark 5–6)
Oven position: near top
Serves: 4–6

Imperial

Crumb mixture:
6 oz. white breadcrumbs
3 oz. butter
salt
pepper
Salmon filling:
medium-sized can pink or red
    salmon
1 oz. butter
1 oz. flour
½ pint milk
juice of ½ lemon
1 egg yolk
¼ peeled cucumber
seasoning
To garnish:
chopped parsley

Metric

Crumb mixture:
150 g. white breadcrumbs
75 g. butter
salt
pepper
Salmon filling:
medium-sized can pink or red
    salmon
25 g. butter
25 g. flour
250 ml. milk
juice of ½ lemon
1 egg yolk
¼ peeled cucumber
seasoning
To garnish:
chopped parsley

1. Fry breadcrumbs gently in butter until golden brown. Season lightly.
2. Drain and flake the salmon.
3. Melt the butter in a pan, add flour and cook for a few minutes without browning.
4. Remove from heat and add the milk gradually.
5. Return to heat, bring to the boil and allow the sauce to thicken, stirring continuously.
6. Remove from heat.
7. Add lemon juice and beat in the egg yolk.
8. Add salmon.
9. Heat for a further 2 minutes without boiling.
10. Add diced cucumber and seasoning.
11. Arrange layers of salmon and breadcrumbs in a heated dish, finishing with a layer of breadcrumbs.
12. Bake for 15 minutes. Serve sprinkled with parsley.

Variation

Use tuna or shellfish instead of salmon.

Boiled silverside with savoury dumplings

Cooking time: see stage 3
Preparation time: 10 minutes
Main cooking utensil: large saucepan
Serves: 6–8

Imperial	Metric
3–4 lb. salt beef or silverside	1½–2 kg. salt beef or silverside
water	water
1 large onion	1 large onion
1 large carrot	1 large carrot
bay leaf	bay leaf
Dumplings:	*Dumplings:*
4 oz. flour (with plain flour use 1 teaspoon baking powder)	100 g. flour (with plain flour use 1 teaspoon baking powder)
good pinch salt	good pinch salt
2 oz. shredded suet	50 g. shredded suet
½–1 tablespoon chopped herbs	½–1 tablespoon chopped herbs
water to mix	water to mix

1. Soak the beef overnight in cold water.
2. Put into fresh cold water, bring to the boil, add onion, carrot, bay leaf.
3. Simmer very gently in a covered pan, allowing 30 minutes to the lb. (½ kg.) and 30 minutes over.
4. To make the dumplings, sieve the flour and salt, add suet and herbs and mix with enough water to form a sticky dough.
5. Roll into balls with floured hands.
6. Add the dumplings to the stock 15–20 minutes before the end of the cooking time.
7. Lift the meat from the stock, arrange the dumplings round. Serve a little unthickened stock in a sauceboat.

Note: Salted meat shrinks so allow a good 8 oz. (200 g.) per person.

Variation

Dumplings may be varied by adding 1–2 teaspoons grated onion. Enough whole onions and whole or sliced carrots to serve each person may be added approximately 40–50 minutes before the end of the cooking time. If you wish to serve the meat cold, allow it to cool in the stock. This helps to keep it moist.

Roast beef

Cooking time: see stages 1, 2, 3, 4
Preparation time: few minutes
Main cooking utensil: roasting tin
Oven temperature: hot (425–450°F., 220–230°C., Gas Mark 7–8); for slow roasting very moderate (325–350°F., 170–180°C., Gas Mark 3–4)
Oven position: above centre

Joints to choose for roasting :
sirloin
ribs
fillet
aitch-bone (good quality)
topside (better with slow roasting)
brisket (only suitable for slow roasting)
rump

1. Weigh the meat – cooking time depends on this. For under-done ('rare'), allow 15 minutes cooking time per lb. (450 g.) and 15 minutes over. If slow roasting allow 30 minutes per lb. and 30 minutes over.

For medium-done – i.e., well-done on outside, less well done in centre – allow nearly 20 minutes per lb. and 20 minutes over. If slow roasting allow 35 minutes per lb. and 35 minutes over.

For well-done allow a good 20 or even 25 minutes per lb. and 20 minutes over; if slow roasting, nearly 40 minutes per lb. and 40 minutes over.

If using a covered roasting tin or foil allow an extra 20 minutes cooking time or 25°F. (14°C.) higher temperature or one mark higher on a gas cooker. After about 45 minutes the heat can be reduced to moderately hot (400°F., 200°C., Gas Mark 6). This does not apply when slow roasting. Meat that has been frozen is often better if roasted more slowly.

2. To prepare for roasting, season the joint lightly and add a very little fat over the lean part of the meat.

3. Roast the meat as described in stage 1.

4. To make the gravy, drain all but 1 tablespoon fat from the tin. Stir in 1 tablespoon flour or flour and gravy flavouring, cook for several minutes making sure all the sediment is scraped up, then gradually add ½ pint (250 ml.) brown stock, bring to the boil, cook for a few minutes, and strain. Serve with Yorkshire pudding and roast potatoes (see next recipe).

Yorkshire pudding

Cooking time: 15 minutes or 35 minutes
Preparation time: 10 minutes
Main cooking utensil: small patty tins or Yorkshire pudding tin
Oven temperature: hot to very hot (425–475°F., 220–240°C.. Gas
   Mark 7–9)
Oven position: towards top of oven
Serves: 4

Imperial	Metric
4 oz. plain flour	100 g. plain flour
pinch salt	pinch salt
1 egg	1 egg
$\frac{1}{2}$ pint milk or milk and water	250 ml. milk or milk and water
$\frac{1}{2}$–1 oz. fat	15–25 g. fat

1. Sieve flour and salt into a basin.

2. Add the egg and beat well, then beat in enough liquid to give a stiff batter. Allow to stand for a few minutes, then gradually beat in the remainder of the liquid.

3. Either rub patty tins with the fat or put a knob into a larger tin and heat for a few minutes in the oven.

4. It is a good idea to raise the temperature of the oven by 25°F., (14°C.) or one mark with a gas cooker, so the pudding is cooked very quickly.

5. Give batter a final whisk, put into a tin or tins. Bake small puddings for a shorter time; the larger one until firm and brown.

6. Alternatively, lift the meat on to a trivet and pour off all fat but 1 tablespoon, add batter, return meat and batter to oven.

Roast potatoes

Use a little extra fat with the beef. Dry the potatoes, put in hot fat, roast for approximately 45 minutes.

Roast lamb with rosemary

Cooking time: see stage 5
Main cooking utensils: rack, roasting tin
Oven temperature: hot (425–450°F., 220°–230°C., Gas Mark 7–8)
Oven position: above centre
Serves: 6

Imperial	Metric
2 oz. butter	50 g. butter
small leg of lamb	small leg of lamb
seasoning	seasoning
rosemary	rosemary
clove garlic (optional)	clove garlic (optional)
2 lb. potatoes	1 kg. potatoes
To garnish:	*To garnish:*
sprigs rosemary	sprigs rosemary

1. Spread butter over lamb and season well.
2. Stick rosemary leaves into the fat of the meat.
3. Insert a clove of garlic near the bone if you like.
4. Place the joint on a rack in a meat tin.
5. Roast for 20 minutes to the lb. (450 g.) and 20 minutes over.
6. Peel potatoes and cut into $\frac{1}{2}$-inch (1-cm.) thick slices.
7. Place them under the meat after it has been cooking for 30 minutes.
8. Baste joint from time to time.
9. When cooked, garnish with sprigs of rosemary. Serve with roast onions or leeks in a white sauce or tossed in butter.

Variation

Roast meat more slowly, i.e., 30 minutes per lb. and 30 minutes over, in a moderately hot oven (375–400°F., 190–200°C., Gas Mark 5–6).

Irish stew

Cooking time: 2 hours 10 minutes
Preparation time: 20 minutes
Main cooking utensil: large saucepan
Serves: 4

Imperial	**Metric**
1½ lb. neck of lamb	¾ kg. neck of lamb
12 oz. onions	350 g. onions
seasoning	seasoning
¾ pint water	450 ml. water
1 lb. medium-sized potatoes	½ kg. medium-sized potatoes
To garnish:	*To garnish:*
chopped parsley	chopped parsley

1. Divide the meat into neat pieces.
2. Peel and slice the onions.
3. Put the meat and onions, with seasoning and water to cover, into a saucepan.
4. Bring to the boil, remove any scum, then lower the heat and simmer gently for approximately 1½ hours.
5. Add the whole potatoes and cook for a further 30–40 minutes.
6. Add a little extra seasoning. Lift on to a hot dish and garnish with chopped parsley.

Note: Choose middle or scrag end of neck. For a more luxurious dish use best end of neck or even loin chops.

Variations

To give a thicker gravy, add 2 potatoes at the beginning of the cooking time so that they break up and thicken the stock. To cook this dish in a casserole, allow approximately the same time in the centre of a very moderate oven (325–350°F., 170–180°C., Gas Mark 3–4), adding the potatoes approximately 45 minutes before the end of the cooking time.

Steak and kidney pudding

Cooking time: minimum of 4 hours
Preparation time: 20 minutes
Main cooking utensils: 2-pint (1-litre) pudding basin, steamer,
saucepan, greaseproof paper, cloth
Serves: 4

Imperial	Metric
Suet crust:	*Suet crust:*
8 oz. flour (with plain flour use 1 teaspoon baking powder)	200 g. flour (with plain flour use 1 teaspoon baking powder)
4 oz. shredded suet	100 g. shredded suet
seasoning	seasoning
water to mix	water to mix
Filling:	*Filling:*
1 lb. stewing steak	400 g. stewing steak
2–3 lamb's kidneys or 4 oz. ox kidney	2–3 lamb's kidneys or 100 g. ox kidney
$\frac{1}{2}$ oz. flour	15 g. flour
seasoning	seasoning
water or stock	water or stock

1. To make the suet crust, mix all the dry ingredients together and add enough water to make a firm dough.
2. Line the greased basin with most of the pastry, retaining enough for the cover.
3. Cut the meat into small pieces.
4. Skin, core and chop the kidneys.
5. Mix the meats well together and put into the lined basin, sprinkling each layer with flour and seasoning.
6. Add enough water or stock nearly to fill the basin.
7. Put on the pastry lid, damp the edges and seal well together.
8. Cover with greased greaseproof paper and cloth, or a cloth dipped in boiling water and floured. Leave room for the pastry to swell.
9. Steam for a minimum of 4 hours. Serve with thickened gravy and green vegetables.

Variations
Add finely chopped onions; a few mushrooms; or any vegetable.

Shepherd's pie

Cooking time: 25–30 minutes plus time to cook potatoes
Preparation time: 15 minutes
Main cooking utensils: 1½- to 2-pint (¾- to 1-litre) pie or ovenproof
   dish
Oven temperature: moderately hot (375–400°F., 190–200°C., Gas
Mark 5–6)
Oven position: centre
Serves: 4

Imperial	Metric
12 oz. cooked beef	300 g. cooked beef
1–2 oz. fat	25–50 g. fat
1–2 onions	1–2 onions
2 large tomatoes	2 large tomatoes
1 oz. flour	25 g. flour
$\frac{1}{3}$ pint brown stock	175 ml. brown stock
1 teaspoon chopped parsley	1 teaspoon chopped parsley
pinch mixed herbs	pinch mixed herbs
seasoning	seasoning
Topping:	*Topping:*
1–1$\frac{1}{2}$ lb. creamed potatoes	400–600 g. creamed potatoes
$\frac{1}{2}$–1 oz. margarine	15–25 g. margarine
To garnish:	*To garnish:*
sliced tomato	sliced tomato
parsley	parsley

1. Mince the beef or chop it finely.
2. Heat the fat and fry the sliced onions and tomatoes in it until tender.
3. Stir in the flour and cook for several minutes.
4. Gradually add the stock, cooking until a thick sauce is formed.
5. Add the meat, parsley and herbs and season well.
6. Put into the pie dish, top with the well creamed potatoes and dot with small pieces of margarine. Bake for 25–30 minutes until crisp and brown. Serve topped with sliced tomato and parsley.

Note: This same recipe can be used with flaked cooked fish, using brown stock as above.

Variations

A little grated cheese may be put on the top before browning. The cooked potatoes may be sliced instead of creamed. Sliced hard-boiled egg may be put over the beef mixture.

Savoury minced steak with soufflé topping

Cooking time: 40 minutes
Preparation time: 20 minutes
Main cooking utensils: frying pan, overproof dish, basin over hot
   water
Oven temperature: moderate (375°F., 190°C., Gas Mark 5)
Oven position: centre
Serves: 4

Imperial	Metric
1 small green pepper	1 small green pepper
1 small onion	1 small onion
2 oz. mushrooms	50 g. mushrooms
2 tomatoes	2 tomatoes
1 tablespoon oil	1 tablespoon oil
16-oz. can minced steak	450-g. can minced steak
pinch of oregano or mixed herbs	pinch of oregano or mixed herbs
seasoning	seasoning
Soufflé topping:	*Soufflé topping:*
2 oz. finely grated Cheddar cheese	50 g. finely grated Cheddar cheese
3 tablespoons evaporated milk	3 tablespoons evaporated milk
2 eggs	2 eggs
salt	salt
pinch cayenne pepper	pinch cayenne pepper
To garnish:	*To garnish:*
sprig of parsley	sprig of parsley

1. Chop the pepper, removing seeds and core, skin and chop the onion, skin and slice the mushrooms and tomatoes.
2. Heat the oil and lightly fry all the vegetables until onion is golden brown.
3. Place the minced steak in the ovenproof dish, top with the vegetables.
4. Sprinkle seasonings on top.
5. Make the soufflé by melting the cheese in the evaporated milk in a basin over hot water. Allow to cool slightly.
6. Stir in the egg yolks.
7. Whisk egg whites stiffly, then fold in the cheese mixture. Season.
8. Place on top of the meat and vegetables.
9. Bake until the soufflé is well risen and lightly browned, 20—25 minutes. Serve at once, garnished with parsley.

Hunter's roll

Cooking time: 2 hours
Preparation time: 20 minutes
Main cooking utensils: saucepan, steamer
Serves: 4–6

Imperial	Metric
8 oz. self-raising flour (or plain flour and 2 level teaspoons baking powder)	200 g. self-raising flour (or plain flour and 2 level teaspoons baking powder)
$\frac{1}{2}$ level teaspoon salt	$\frac{1}{2}$ level teaspoon salt
4 oz. shredded suet	100 g. shredded suet
$\frac{1}{4}$ pint water	125 ml. water
4–6 oz. bacon	100–150 g. bacon
6 oz. calves' liver	150 g. calves' liver
1 level teaspoon chopped parsley	1 level teaspoon chopped parsley

1. Sieve flour and salt. Add suet.

2. Mix with water to a soft but not sticky dough. Knead lightly on a floured board, till smooth. Roll out into an oblong approximately 10 inches by 12 inches (25 cm. by 30 cm.).

3. Chop bacon and liver finely.

4. Mix with parsley and spread to within $\frac{1}{2}$ inch (1 cm.) of the edges of the pastry.

5. Moisten edges with water, then roll up loosely, as for a Swiss roll.

6. Wrap well in greased greaseproof paper and steam over boiling water for 2 hours. Serve with a thickened gravy and vegetables.

Note: If you have any left over you can wrap it in fresh paper and resteam it.

Variations

Baked roll: Cook for approximately $1-1\frac{1}{4}$ hours in the centre of a moderately hot oven (400°F., 200°C., Gas Mark 6), reduce heat after 30 minutes.

Add 1–2 sliced onions.

Omit the liver and add extra vegetables.

Spaghetti bolognese

Cooking time: sauce 1 hour, spaghetti 15 minutes
Preparation time: 30 minutes
Main cooking utensils: 2 saucepans
Serves: 4 as a main course or 8 as a starter

Imperial
8 oz. spaghetti
Parmesan cheese
Sauce:
1 oz. butter
1 tablespoon olive oil
2 oz. mushrooms
1 onion
1 carrot
6–8 oz. minced raw beef
1 small can concentrated
   tomato purée or tomatoes
seasoning
½ pint good stock if using
   canned tomatoes, slightly
   more for tomato purée
¼ pint red wine

Metric
200 g. spaghetti
Parmesan cheese
Sauce:
25 g. butter
1 tablespoon olive oil
50 g. mushrooms
1 onion
1 carrot
150–200 g. minced raw beef
1 small can concentrated
   tomato purée or tomatoes
seasoning
250 ml. good stock if using
   canned tomatoes, slightly
   more for tomato purée
125 ml. red wine

1. Cook the sauce first as it takes longer than the spaghetti. Heat the butter and oil in a pan and fry the finely chopped mushrooms, shredded onion and shredded carrot.
2. Stir in the meat, simmer gently, then add the rest of the ingredients.
3. Continue to cook until thickened and a rich flavour, stirring from time to time.
4. Put spaghetti on to cook in boiling salted water.
5. Arrange the drained spaghetti on a hot dish and pour over the sauce. Serve with grated Parmesan cheese.

Variation

For an alternative sauce heat together 1 2¼-oz. (50-g.) can tomato purée, 1 15-oz. (400-g.) can minced steak and ¼ teaspoon mixed herbs or oregano.

Chili con carne

Cooking time: 50 minutes plus time to cook beans
Preparation time: 25 minutes plus time to soak beans
Main cooking utensil: large saucepan
Serves: 3–4

Imperial	Metric
2 oz. margarine	50 g. margarine
1 large onion	1 large onion
1 green pepper (optional)	1 green pepper (optional)
2 sticks celery	2 sticks celery
1 tablespoon chilli powder	1 tablespoon chilli powder
8 oz. soaked and cooked haricot beans	200 g. soaked and cooked haricot beans
$\frac{1}{2}$ teaspoon salt	$\frac{1}{2}$ teaspoon salt
1 lb. minced raw beef	400 g. minced raw beef
8 oz. tomatoes or $\frac{1}{2}$ pint tomato pulp	200 g. tomatoes or 250 ml. tomato pulp
$\frac{1}{4}$ pint water or water and a beef stock cube	125 ml. water or water and a beef stock cube

1. Heat the margarine in the pan.
2. Chop the onion finely, then chop the pepper. Leave a few rings for garnish and cut the remainder of the flesh into neat small pieces, discarding core and seeds.
3. Chop celery finely.
4. Put into the margarine and fry gently until just tender.
5. Add in all the other ingredients.
6. Bring to the boil, stir very well, then lower heat and allow to simmer gently for approximately 35 minutes.
7. The pan should be covered tightly, but halfway through cooking, stir well, then add a very little more water if wished — but this must be a firm mixture.
8. Tip into a hot dish and serve with a vegetable, for example green beans.

Note: Chilli powder is extremely hot so be sparing with it until you know how hot you like this dish.

Variation
Instead of chilli powder use $\frac{1}{2}$–1 teaspoon cayenne and 2 teaspoons paprika pepper.

Fried chicken

Cooking time: 15–20 minutes
Preparation time: 5–8 minutes
Main cooking utensil: either large frying pan or deep fat pan with
    basket
Serves: 4

Imperial	Metric
4 joints of young chicken	4 joints of young chicken
To coat	*To coat*
1 oz. flour	25 g. flour
seasoning	seasoning
OR	OR
1 egg	1 egg
little water	little water
3 tablespoons crisp breadcrumbs (raspings)	3 tablespoons crisp breadcrumbs (raspings)
For frying:	*For frying:*
3 oz. butter, fat or oil for shallow frying	75 g. butter, fat or oil for shallow frying
OR	OR
at least 1 lb. fat or 1 pint oil for deep frying	at least 450 g. fat or 550 ml. oil for deep frying

1. Put the flour and seasoning on to a plate, on greaseproof paper or in a bag.
2. Either turn the chicken (very well dried) in it or drop it into the bag and shake well until coated.
3. To coat in egg and breadcrumbs, beat egg on a plate – a little water can be added to make it go further.
4. Brush chicken with this, roll in breadcrumbs until evenly coated. Shake off surplus before cooking.
5. To shallow fry, heat fat in pan.
6. Add chicken cook for 4 minutes, then turn and cook for a further 4 minutes. Lower heat, cook for a further 10–12 minutes, turning once or twice.
7. To deep fry, heat oil or fat until a cube of day-old bread turns golden brown in $\frac{1}{2}$–1 minute. Put in chicken and cook for approximately 12–15 minutes; lower heat when it goes in.
8. Whether shallow or deep fried, drain on crumpled tissue or kitchen paper. Serve with vegetables or salad.

Chicken casserole with dumplings

Cooking time: 1 hour
Preparation time: 25 minutes
Main cooking utensils: large saucepan, casserole
Oven temperature: moderate (375°F., 190°C., Gas Mark 5)
Oven position: centre
Serves: 4

Imperial	Metric
4 joints frying chicken	4 joints frying chicken
seasoning	seasoning
1 oz. cornflour	25 g. cornflour
2 tablespoons corn oil	2 tablespoons corn oil
3–4 small carrots, diced	3–4 small carrots, diced
1 onion, sliced	1 onion, sliced
1 chicken bouillon cube	1 chicken bouillon cube
1 pint boiling water	550 ml. boiling water
1 small can tomato purée	1 small can tomato purée
2 tablespoons white wine	2 tablespoons white wine
(optional)	(optional)
1 bay leaf	1 bay leaf
4 oz. mushrooms, sliced	100 g. mushrooms, sliced
few cooked green peas	few cooked green peas
Dumplings:	*Dumplings:*
3 oz. plain flour	75 g. plain flour
½ oz. cornflour	15 g. cornflour
pinch salt	pinch salt
1 level teaspoon baking powder	1 level teaspoon baking powder
1 tablespoon corn oil	1 tablespoon corn oil
3 good tablespoons milk	3 good tablespoons milk
To garnish:	*To garnish:*
chopped parsley	chopped parsley

1. Coat the chicken joints with the seasoned cornflour, and brown in the hot corn oil.

2. Transfer to a casserole with the carrots and onion.

3. Dissolve the chicken cube in boiling water, mix in the tomato purée.

4. Add the wine and bay leaf and pour over the chicken and vegetables in the casserole.

5. Cover tightly and cook in the oven for approximately 30 minutes.

6. Meanwhile make the dumplings. Sieve the dry ingredients, add oil, and enough milk to form a soft dough. Form into balls.

7. Add mushrooms and peas to casserole and continue cooking for a further 30 minutes. At the same time, boil the dumplings in salted water for 15–20 minutes or cook in a steamer over boiling water for 30 minutes.

8. Arrange cooked dumplings on the stew, and sprinkle with chopped parsley.

Kentish chicken pudding

Cooking time: 2½–3 hours
Preparation time: 20 minutes
Main cooking utensils: 2-pint (1-litre pudding basin, steamer,
   saucepan, foil
Serves: 4

Imperial	**Metric**
Suet crust:	*Suet crust:*
8 oz. self-raising flour (with plain flour use 2 level teaspoons baking powder)	200 g. self-raising flour (with plain flour use 2 level teaspoons baking powder)
½ level teaspoon salt	½ level teaspoon salt
3 oz. shredded suet	75 g. shredded suet
¼ pint less 1 tablespoon water	110 ml. water
Filling:	*Filling:*
8 oz. salt pork belly	200 g. salt pork belly
4 small chicken joints or 12 oz. uncooked chicken meat	4 small chicken joints or 300 g. uncooked chicken meat
1 large onion, chopped	1 large onion, chopped
seasoning	seasoning
1 heaped tablespoon chopped parsley	1 heaped tablespoon chopped parsley

1. Sieve together the flour and salt, mix in suet and add water.
2. Mix to a soft dough, knead until smooth.
3. Cut off a third of the pastry for a lid and roll out the rest.
4. Carefully line a basin with pastry.
5. Cut the pork into 1-inch (2½-cm.) cubes.
6. Put into the pastry-lined basin with the chicken joints, onion, seasoning and parsley.
7. Fill the basin three-quarters full with water and put on pastry lid.
8. Cover with a double layer of greased greaseproof paper or foil.
9. Cook for the time given. Serve with a green vegetable.

Variation
Add mixed vegetables instead of pork.

Chicken and mushroom pie

Cooking time: 35 minutes
Preparation time: 30 minutes plus time for pastry to stand
Main cooking utensil: 2-pint (1-litre) pie dish
Oven temperature: hot (425–450°F., 220–230°C., Gas Mark 7–8),
   then moderate (375°F., 190°C., Gas Mark 5)
Oven position: just above centre
Serves: 6

Imperial	**Metric**
Rough puff pastry:	*Rough puff pastry:*
3 oz. cooking fat mixed with 3 oz. margarine	75 g. cooking fat mixed with 75 g. margarine
8 oz. plain flour	200 g. plain flour
pinch salt	pinch salt
1 teaspoon lemon juice	1 teaspoon lemon juice
cold water	cold water
Filling:	*Filling:*
2 oz. butter	50 g. butter
2 oz. flour	50 g. flour
1 pint milk	550 ml. milk
seasoning	seasoning
8–12 oz. cooked chicken	200–300 g. cooked chicken
4 oz. mushrooms	100 g. mushrooms
Glaze:	*Glaze:*
1 egg	1 egg
1 tablespoon milk	1 tablespoon milk

1. Make the pastry. Cut the fat into the sieved flour and salt, mix to a soft dough with the lemon juice and water, put on a floured board.

2. Roll to an oblong, fold in three, seal ends and turn, repeat for further three times. Cool well before using.

3. Make the filling. Heat the butter, stir in the flour and cook for several minutes, then gradually blend in the milk. Bring to the boil and cook until thickened and smooth; stir well.

4. Add seasoning, chopped chicken, sliced uncooked mushrooms.

5. Put into the pie dish, cover with pastry.

6. Seal edges and decorate with leaves of pastry. Glaze with egg and milk.

7. Bake for 15 minutes in a hot oven, then lower the heat to moderate for a further 20 minutes until the pastry is brown and filling hot. Serve hot or cold with vegetables or a green salad.

Variation

Use a brown sauce instead of a white sauce and add mixed diced cooked vegetables instead of mushrooms.

Liver and bacon hot pot

Cooking time: 2 hours
Preparation time: 15 minutes plus overnight soaking of prunes
Main cooking utensil: casserole
Oven temperature: very moderate to moderate (350–375°F., 180–190°C., Gas Mark 4–5)
Oven position: centre
Serves: 4

Imperial	Metric
1 lb. leeks	400 g. leeks
8 oz. tomatoes	200 g. tomatoes
8 rashers streaky bacon	8 rashers streaky bacon
1 lb. sliced lamb's liver	400 g. sliced lamb's liver
12 prunes soaked overnight in $\frac{3}{4}$ pint stock or water and a beef stock cube	12 prunes soaked overnight in 400 ml. stock or water and a beef stock cube
seasoning	seasoning

1. Clean and slice the leeks, peel and quarter the tomatoes.
2. Remove rind from the bacon rashers and roll up tightly.
3. Arrange sliced liver, leeks, tomatoes and drained prunes in a casserole, seasoning each layer.
4. Top with bacon rolls.
5. Pour in the reserved soaking stock almost to cover the contents.
6. Cover and cook for $1\frac{1}{2}$ hours.
7. Remove lid and continue cooking until the bacon rolls are golden brown and the liver is tender. Serve hot with jacket or creamed potatoes and a green vegetable.

Variation

Thicken stock with 1 oz. (25 g.) flour at stage 5, heat in a pan until smooth, then add to the casserole. Ox liver can be used in this dish. Slice it very thinly, and allow approximately $2\frac{1}{2}$–3 hours cooking time. Use onions instead of leeks.

Spare ribs of pork with barbecue sauce

Cooking time: 20 minutes
Preparation time: 15 minutes
Main cooking utensils: grill pan, saucepan
Serves: 4

Imperial	Metric
8 spare ribs of pork	8 spare ribs of pork
1 oz. butter	25 g. butter
seasoning	seasoning
Barbecue sauce:	*Barbecue sauce:*
1 oz. butter	25 g. butter
2 sliced onions	2 sliced onions
1 clove garlic	1 clove garlic
4 oz. mushrooms	100 g. mushrooms
medium-sized can tomatoes	medium-sized can tomatoes
1 teaspoon Worcestershire sauce	1 teaspoon Worcestershire sauce
1 teaspoon made mustard	1 teaspoon made mustard
$\frac{1}{2}$ teaspoon mixed herbs	$\frac{1}{2}$ teaspoon mixed herbs
$\frac{1}{2}$ teaspoon castor sugar	$\frac{1}{2}$ teaspoon castor sugar
seasoning	seasoning
To garnish:	*To garnish:*
watercress	watercress

1. Brush the spare ribs with melted butter and season well.
2. Grill for 15–20 minutes, turning once or twice and lowering heat after 10 minutes.
3. Melt butter in a pan.
4. Gently fry the onions and crushed clove of garlic, add chopped mushrooms and fry for a few minutes.
5. Add tomatoes, Worcestershire sauce, mustard, herbs, sugar and seasoning.
6. Simmer for about 10 minutes.
7. Pour over chops and garnish with fresh watercress. Serve with boiled carrots and creamed or jacket potatoes.

Variation
Use 6 large skinned fresh tomatoes and $\frac{1}{4}$ pint (125 ml.) stock instead of canned tomatoes.

Sausage meat roll

Cooking time: 1 hour
Preparation time: 15 minutes
Main cooking utensil: flat baking sheet or tin
Oven temperature: moderate (375°F., 190°C., Gas Mark 5) then
  very moderate (350°F., 180°C., Gas Mark 4) if necessary
Oven position: centre
Serves: 4–6

Imperial	Metric
6 oz. self-raising flour (or plain flour with 1 teaspoon baking powder)	150 g. self-raising flour (or plain flour with 1 teaspoon baking powder)
pinch salt	pinch salt
3 oz. shredded suet	75 g. shredded suet
water to mix	water to mix
Filling:	*Filling:*
12 oz. sausage meat	300 g. sausage meat
2 chopped apples or 2–4 chopped prunes or 3 skinned chopped tomatoes	2 chopped apples or 2–4 chopped prunes or 3 skinned chopped tomatoes
2 chopped onions	2 chopped onions
seasoning	seasoning
1 teaspoon powdered sage	1 teaspoon powdered sage
To garnish:	*To garnish:*
2 tomatoes	2 tomatoes

1. Sieve the flour or flour and baking powder and salt.

2. Add the suet and enough water to make a rolling consistency.

3. Roll into a neat oblong.

4. Mix the sausage meat with the chopped apples or prunes or tomatoes, onions, seasoning and sage.

5. Spread over the suet crust, damp edges and roll like a Swiss roll.

6. Lift on to a baking tin.

7. Bake until crisp and golden brown, lowering heat after 30 minutes if necessary.

8. Garnish with sliced tomatoes. Serve hot, cut in slices.

Variation

Wrap lightly in a floured cloth or greased foil and steam for $1\frac{1}{2}$ hours.

Bacon and sausage plait

Cooking time: 30 minutes
Preparation time: 30 minutes
Main cooking utensils: baking tray or baking sheet
Oven temperature: very hot (475°F., 240°C., Gas Mark 9), then hot
  (425–450°F., 220–230°C., Gas Mark 7–8)
Oven position: centre
Serves: 6

Imperial	Metric
Puff pastry:	*Puff pastry:*
6 oz. flour	150 g. flour
salt	salt
little lemon juice	little lemon juice
water	water
6 oz. butter	150 g. butter
Filling:	*Filling:*
8 oz. pork sausage meat	200 g. pork sausage meat
8 oz. chopped cooked bacon	200 g. chopped cooked bacon
2 roughly chopped hard-boiled eggs	2 roughly chopped hard-boiled eggs
1 teaspoon sage or basil	1 teaspoon sage or basil
seasoning	seasoning
Glaze:	*Glaze:*
1 egg	1 egg
little salt	little salt

1. Sieve flour and salt. Make into an elastic dough with lemon juice and water. Roll out to oblong shape. Put on butter, fold dough over this, turn, seal edges. Give seven rollings and seven foldings, allowing pastry to rest in a cool place.
2. Roll pastry out to a 10-inch (25-cm.) square.
3. Mix all the ingredients together for the filling and place down the centre, leaving equal sides of empty pastry. Cut sides obliquely in ½-inch (1-cm.) strips (rather like a fish fin) and brush with beaten egg. Lift alternate strips over the sausage mixture to form a roll resembling a plait.
4. Brush with egg and sprinkle with salt.
5. Bake for approximately 15 minutes in a very hot oven, then lower heat for a further 15 minutes. Serve hot or cold, with a vegetable or salad.

Variation
Add mushrooms instead of eggs. Use frozen puff pastry if you have no time to make your own.

Savoury bacon pudding

Cooking time: 3 hours
Preparation time: 25 minutes
Main cooking utensils: 1½- to 2-pint (¾- to 1-litre) basin, greaseproof
   paper or foil, steamer, saucepan.
Serves: 4–5

Imperial

Suet crust pastry:
8 oz. self-raising flour
pinch salt
4 oz. shredded suet
cold water to mix
Filling:
8–12 oz. streaky bacon
1–2 chopped onions
1–2 chopped tomatoes
1–2 diced carrots
small piece sliced cucumber
   (optional) or diced marrow
   (optional)
little chopped parsley
water
pepper

Metric

Suet crust pastry:
200 g. self-raising flour
pinch salt
100 g. shredded suet
cold water to mix
Filling:
200–300 g. streaky bacon
1–2 chopped onions
1–2 chopped tomatoes
1–2 diced carrots
small piece sliced cucumber
   (optional) or diced marrow
   (optional)
little chopped parsley
water
pepper

1. Sieve the flour and salt, add the suet and enough water to make a rolling consistency.

2. Roll out on a floured board, use two-thirds to line a 1½- to 2-pint (¾- to 1-litre) basin.

3. Fill with the diced bacon, vegetables, parsley and a very little water. Add pepper, no salt should be needed unless using green bacon.

4. Roll out remaining suet crust to form a lid, press over the top of the mixture, cover with greased greaseproof paper or foil.

5. Steam over boiling water for the time given. When cooked, either turn out or serve from the basin. Garnish with watercress if you like.

Variation

Diced meat or poultry could be used in place of the bacon. Fruit and sugar may be used in place of meat in this type of pastry.

Bacon savoury

Cooking time: 40 minutes
Preparation time: 15 minutes
Main cooking utensils: frying pan, ovenproof or pie dish, large pipe
and cloth bag
Oven temperature: moderate (375°F., 190°C., Gas Mark 4–5)
Oven position: centre
Serves: 4

Imperial	Metric
3 chopped spring onions or a little grated onion	3 chopped spring onions or a little grated onion
3 eggs	3 eggs
½ pint milk	250 ml. milk
½ teaspoon powdered sage seasoning	½ teaspoon powdered sage seasoning
1½ lb. mashed potatoes	700 g. mashed potatoes
8 oz. diced bacon (rashers cut from gammon, back, prime collar, or streaky bacon)	200 g. diced bacon (rashers cut from gammon, back, prime collar, or streaky bacon)

1. Fry the onion until crisp.
2. Beat the eggs and add milk, sage and onion. Season well.
3. Grease an ovenproof dish and pipe mashed potato round the edge. Put the bacon in the centre of dish, pour over the egg mixture and sprinkle the top with cheese.
4. Bake for about 30 minutes until set, with the potato border browned. Serve with baked tomatoes.

To pipe potatoes

Have the potato warm – it pipes more readily. Put the pipe into the bag. Half fill the piping bag with potato and press firmly. For a flowing edge, hold the bag at an angle like a pen. For rosettes hole the bag upright.

To make Duchesse potatoes, add an egg and margarine to the potatoes, but no milk.

Variation

Add 2 oz. (50 g.) chopped mushrooms instead of onion.

Cheese and onion pie

Cooking time: 35 minutes
Preparation time: 25 minutes
Main cooking utensils: 8-inch (20-cm.) pie plate, frying pan
Oven temperature: moderately hot (375–400°F., 190–200°C., Gas
   Mark 5–6)
Oven position: centre
Serves: 4–6

Imperial

Cheese pastry:
8 oz. plain flour
pinch salt
shake pepper
pinch dry mustard
3 oz. butter
4 oz. grated Cheddar cheese
2½ tablespoons cold water
Filling:
2 oz. butter
4 large sliced onions
6 oz. grated Cheddar cheese
seasoning
2 teaspoons Worcestershire
   sauce
Glaze:
little milk

Metric

Cheese pastry:
200 g. plain flour
pinch salt
shake pepper
pinch dry mustard
75 g. butter
100 g. grated Cheddar cheese
2½ tablespoons cold water
Filling:
50 g. butter
4 large sliced onions
150 g. grated Cheddar cheese
seasoning
2 teaspoons Worcestershire
   sauce
Glaze:
little milk

1. Sieve flour, salt, pepper and mustard into a mixing bowl.
2. Rub in butter and add cheese.
3. Add enough water to make a firm dough.
4. Melt butter in frying pan and fry onions until soft.
5. Divide pastry into two and roll out each half to fit a pie plate.
6. Line the pie plate with one half of the pastry and prick the bottom with a fork.
7. Pile in alternate layers of cheese and cooked onion, beginning and ending with cheese; season each layer.
8. Sprinkle Worcestershire sauce over, cover with the second round of pastry.
9. Seal and flute the edge; make a hole in the centre; decorate with leaves and a rose made from the remaining pastry; glaze.
10. Bake until crisp and golden. Serve hot with vegetables or cold with salad.

Note: Cheese pastry stores well as crumbs (stage 2), or wrapped in foil.

Variation
Use 3–4 sliced tomatoes and 2–4 oz. (50–100 g.) sliced mushrooms in place of onions.

Salmon and sweet-corn flan

Cooking time: 25–30 minutes
Preparation time: 25 minutes
Main cooking utensils: 8-inch (20-cm.) flan ring or tin, saucepan
Oven temperature: moderately hot (400°F., 200°C., Gas Mark 6)
Oven position: just above centre
Serves: 4–6

Imperial	Metric
Pastry:	*Pastry:*
3 oz. margarine	75 g. margarine
6 oz. plain flour	150 g. plain flour
pinch salt	pinch salt
1½–2 tablespoons water	1½–2 tablespoons water
Filling:	*Filling:*
1 oz. margarine	25 g. margarine
1 oz. plain flour	25 g. plain flour
½ pint milk	250 ml. milk
1 medium-sized can sweetcorn	1 medium-sized can sweetcorn
1 medium-sized can salmon	1 medium-sized can salmon
finely grated rind of ½ lemon	finely grated rind of ½ lemon
seasoning	seasoning
2 oz. grated Cheddar cheese	50 g. grated Cheddar cheese
To garnish:	*To garnish:*
parsley	parsley

1. Rub margarine into the flour sieved with a pinch of salt until it resembles fine breadcrumbs. Mix with water to form a firm dough.

2. Roll out, line a flan ring placed on baking sheet, trim edges, fill with greaseproof paper and baking beans.

3. Bake 'blind' for 10–15 minutes.

4. Remove beans and paper and continue cooking for a further 10–15 minutes until lightly browned.

5. Melt margarine, stir in flour, cook gently for 2 minutes, remove from the heat.

6. Add milk gradually, beating well.

7. Bring to boil, cook until thick stirring continuously.

8. Remove from the heat, stir in drained sweetcorn, flaked salmon, lemon rind and seasoning and pour into the flan case.

9. Sprinkle with cheese, return to oven or place under hot grill to brown the top. Serve hot, garnish with parsley.

Variation

Serve cold with salad. Put the cold filling into cooled pastry.

Macaroni cheese de luxe

Cooking time: 25–30 minutes
Preparation time: 20 minutes
Main cooking utensils: 2 saucepans, ovenproof dish
Serves: 4

Imperial	Metric
4–6 oz. quick cooking macaroni	100–150 g. quick cooking macaroni
4 rashers bacon	4 rashers bacon
2 small tomatoes	2 small tomatoes
Cheese sauce:	*Cheese sauce:*
1 oz. butter	25 g. butter
1 oz. flour	25 g. flour
½ pint milk	250 ml. milk
seasoning	seasoning
6 oz. grated Cheddar cheese	150 g. grated Cheddar cheese
1 level teaspoon made mustard	1 level teaspoon made mustard
To garnish:	*To garnish:*
triangles of toast	triangles of toast
parsley sprigs	parsley sprigs

1. Cook the macaroni according to the directions on the packet.
2. Meanwhile prepare the cheese sauce. Heat the butter in a pan. Stir in the flour. Cook for 2–3 minutes, stirring well until dry. Remove pan from heat and gradually blend in the milk. Bring to the boil, stirring well, and season.
3. Add the cheese, reserving about 2 tablespoons for topping, and the mustard.
4. Add the cooked, drained macaroni to the sauce and heat together. Do not over-cook.
5. Spoon this mixture into the greased dish.
6. Sprinkle remaining cheese on top.
7. Make small bacon rolls with halved bacon rashers.
8. Put the rolls on a long skewer with the halved tomatoes.
9. Brown under a hot grill at the same time as the macaroni until the rolls are crisp and the cheese golden brown.
10. Garnish with toast triangles and parsley and serve with the bacon and tomato.

Variation
Bake for approximately 30 minutes in a moderate oven (375°F., 190°C., Gas Mark 5). You can use a little extra milk if wished.

Danish barbecued potatoes

Cooking time: 1 hour
Preparation time: 15 minutes
Main cooking utensils: frying pan, baking tin, skewer
Oven temperature: moderately hot (400°F., 200°C., Gas Mark 6)
Serves: 6

Imperial	Metric
6 large potatoes	6 large potatoes
seasoning	seasoning
knob of butter	knob of butter
4 oz. grated cheese	100 g. grated cheese
12 rashers streaky or back bacon	12 rashers streaky or back bacon
1 oz. butter	25 g. butter
1 onion, thinly sliced	1 onion, thinly sliced
3 large tomatoes	3 large tomatoes
mustard	mustard
dash Worcestershire sauce	dash Worcestershire sauce
To garnish:	*To garnish:*
parsley	parsley

1. Cook the potatoes in their jackets until soft.
2. Halve carefully and remove potato pulp.
3. Mash with seasoning, a knob of butter and nearly all the cheese.
4. Pile or pipe back into the potato cases, leaving a large well in the middle.
5. Sprinkle with the rest of the cheese.
6. Make 6 rashers into 12 small bacon rolls, put on to a skewer.
7. Put bacon rolls and potato cases in the oven for about 10 minutes until crisp.
8. Meanwhile, heat the butter in a pan, fry sliced onions until nearly tender, add the rest of the bacon cut in thin strips, fry until cooked.
9. Stir in sliced tomatoes and seasonings, including mustard and Worcestershire sauce.
10. Cook gently to a soft moist mixture.
11. Pile into each potato case.
12. Top with bacon rolls; garnish with parsley.
13. Serve hot. Ideal for a barbecue supper.

Potato burgers

Cooking time: 10 minutes
Preparation time: 15 minutes
Main cooking utensils: frying pan, pastry cutter
Serves: 4

Imperial
1 lb. mashed potato
2 oz. plain flour
seasoning
butter or fat for frying
Filling:
2 oz. finely chopped onion
8 oz. raw minced beef
seasoning

Metric
400 g. mashed potato
50 g. plain flour
seasoning
butter or fat for frying
Filling:
50 g. finely chopped onion
200 g. raw minced beef
seasoning

1. Mix together the mashed potato, flour, salt and pepper.
2. Roll out on a floured surface to a good $\frac{1}{4}$-inch ($\frac{1}{2}$-cm.) thickness and cut into rounds ($2\frac{1}{2}$ inches (6 cm.) to 3 inches ($7\frac{1}{2}$ cm.) in diameter) with a pastry cutter.
3. Fry in a little hot butter or fat until lightly browned on both sides, then lift on to a plate and keep hot.
4. Add the onion to the minced beef and season well. Form into flat rounds the same size as the potato cakes, and fry in a little fat, turning halfway through cooking.
5. Sandwich a burger between two potato cakes and serve piping hot, with pickles, chutney or mustard.

Cheese and vegetable casserole

Cooking time: 1 hour
Preparation time: 30 minutes
Main cooking utensils: saucepans, ovenproof dish
Oven temperature: moderate (375°F., 190°C., Gas Mark 5)
Oven position: above centre
Serves: 4

Imperial	Metric
8 small onions	8 small onions
salt	salt
12 oz. small carrots	300 g. small carrots
1 small swede	1 small swede
medium-sized packet frozen peas or 12 oz. fresh peas	medium-sized packet frozen peas or 300 g. fresh peas
12 oz. potatoes	300 g. potatoes
Sauce:	*Sauce:*
1½ oz. margarine or butter	40 g. margarine or butter
1½ oz. flour	40 g. flour
¾ pint milk	400 ml. milk
seasoning	seasoning
little mustard	little mustard
6 oz. grated cheese	150 g. grated cheese

1. Peel the onions and simmer in salted water for a few minutes.
2. Add carrots and diced swede, and continue cooking until vegetables are nearly tender, then add the peas.
3. Strain vegetables, but keep ¼ pint (125 ml.) of the stock.
4. Meanwhile, cook the potatoes carefully in another pan of salted water until just soft, but not broken; ice thickly.
5. To make the sauce, heat the margarine, stir in the flour and cook for several minutes. Remove from the heat then gradually blend in the milk and the reserved vegetable stock. Bring to the boil and cook until thickened.
6. Add seasoning, mustard and three-quarters of the cheese.
7. Mix the vegetables with this sauce. Put into the oven, top with sliced potatoes and remainder of the cheese. Heat for approximately 20 minutes. Serve hot with a green salad.

Variation
Choose a bigger variety of vegetables, cook these in the casserole rather than a saucepan.

Grilled onion and potato slices

Cooking time: 30 minutes
Preparation time: 10 minutes
Main cooking utensils: saucepan, ovenproof dish
Serves: 4

Imperial	Metric
2 large onions	2 large onions
4 large potatoes	4 large potatoes
salt	salt
Sauce:	*Sauce:*
1 oz. margarine	25 g. margarine
1 oz. flour	25 g. flour
½ pint milk	250 ml. milk
seasoning	seasoning
2–3 oz. grated Cheddar cheese	50–75 g. grated Cheddar cheese

1. Peel both the onions and potatoes.
2. Slice the onions thinly and potatoes thickly, then cook in boiling salted water until just tender; strain.
3. Meanwhile make the sauce. Heat the margarine in a pan, stir in the flour and cook for several minutes, then gradually stir in the milk, bring to the boil and cook, stirring well, until thickened and smooth; season.
4. Arrange vegetables in a dish with the sauce, top with grated cheese and cook under the grill until crisp and brown. Serve for supper, accompanied by grilled tomatoes.

Variations

Instead of making a sauce put the vegetables into the dish with a very little top of the milk and cheese and grill.
Lyonnaise potatoes: Fry half-cooked sliced potatoes and onions in hot fat.

Gipsy potatoes

Cooking time: 1¼ hours
Preparation time: 15 minutes
Main cooking utensils: saucepan or deep frying pan, ovenproof dish
Oven temperature: moderately hot (400°F., 200°C., Gas Mark 6)
Oven position: centre
Serves: 4–5

Imperial	Metric
4 oz. butter	100 g. butter
1½ lb. old or new potatoes	¾ kg. old or new potatoes
seasoning	seasoning
1 lb. tomatoes	½ kg. tomatoes
1 medium onion	1 medium onion
2 oz. soft breadcrumbs	50 g. soft breadcrumbs

1. Melt the butter in a large saucepan.

2. Peel or scrape the potatoes, cut into slices about ⅛ inch (3 mm.) thick.

3. Toss in the butter until each slice is coated, then season to taste.

4. Put the tomatoes into boiling water for ½ minute, then into cold water so that the skins are easily removed.

5. Grate the peeled onion and mix with the tomatoes; season well.

6. Arrange layers of potato and tomato mixture in the dish, ending with potatoes.

7. Sprinkle with breadcrumbs, pour any butter from saucepan over the top.

8. Bake until the potatoes are tender and the top crisp and golden brown. Serve with any meat, fish or vegetable dish.

Note: Keep potatoes in water when peeled to keep them white.

Variations
Add grated cheese to the tomato, etc. Peel the potatoes, cut into slices and put into dish with seasoning, little butter and milk to cover. Bake as above.

Cauliflower cheese

Cooking time: 20 minutes
Preparation time: 12 minutes
Main cooking utensils: 2 saucepans
Serves: 4

Imperial	Metric
1 medium-sized cauliflower	1 medium-sized cauliflower
Coating sauce:	*Coating sauce:*
1 oz. butter or margarine	25 g. butter or margarine
1 oz. flour	25 g. flour
$\frac{1}{2}$ pint liquid (see note)	250 ml. liquid (see note)
seasoning	seasoning
3–4 oz. grated cheese	75–100 g. grated cheese

1. Prepare cauliflower. Remove any hard outer stalks. For quicker cooking, divide into sprigs (this retains more vitamins, but the whole cauliflower looks more impressive).
2. Put into boiling salted water and cook quickly until tender. Strain.
3. Meanwhile prepare the coating sauce. Heat the butter or margarine in a pan. Remove from the heat. Stir in the flour. Cook for 2–3 minutes stirring well until dry. Remove from the heat. Gradually blend in the liquid. Bring to the boil, stirring well, and season.
4. Add the grated cheese to the very hot sauce. Cook gently for 1–2 minutes only.
5. To coat the cauliflower, pour the cheese sauce over the cauliflower, top with a little extra grated cheese if wished, and brown under the grill for a few minutes.

Note: For an ordinary white sauce use $\frac{1}{2}$ pint milk. For sauces to coat vegetables use half milk and half vegetable stock.

Variations
Thin sauce: Proportions as above but 1 pint (500 ml.) liquid.
Panada or binding sauce: As above but $\frac{1}{4}$ pint (125 ml.) liquid.
Parsley sauce: Add chopped parsley to the white sauce.

Onion dumplings

Cooking time: 1 hour 25 minutes
Preparation time: 25 minutes
Main cooking utensils: saucepan, ovenproof dish
Oven temperature: moderate (375–400°F., 190–200°C., Gas Mark 5–6)
Oven position: above centre
Serves: 4

Imperial	Metric
4 large onions	4 large onions
water	water
salt	salt
Cheese pastry:	*Cheese pastry:*
6 oz. plain flour	150 g. plain flour
pinch salt	pinch salt
pinch cayenne pepper	pinch cayenne pepper
pinch dry mustard	pinch dry mustard
2½ oz. butter	65 g. butter
4 oz. finely grated Cheddar cheese	100 g. finely grated Cheddar cheese
1½ tablespoons cold water	1½ tablespoons cold water
1 egg	1 egg
1 oz. grated Cheddar cheese	25 g. grated Cheddar cheese
Cheese sauce:	*Cheese sauce:*
1 oz. margarine	25 g. margarine
1 oz. flour	25 g. flour
½ pint milk	250 ml. milk
seasoning	seasoning
3 oz. grated Cheddar cheese	75 g. grated Cheddar cheese

1. Cook onions in boiling salted water for about 1 hour or until tender.
2. Drain and allow to cool slightly.
3. Prepare the cheese pastry.
4. Sieve the flour, salt, cayenne pepper, and mustard.
5. Rub in the butter, add the finely grated cheese and sufficient cold water to bind.
6. Knead lightly and roll out to a rectangle 6 inches by 12 inches (15 by 30 cm.).
7. Cut eight strips and brush with beaten egg and sprinkle with grated cheese.
8. Put onions into a dish, cover with cheese strips.
9. Bake until pastry is crisp and brown.
10. To make the cheese sauce, heat the margarine in a pan, stir in the flour, and cook for several minutes.
11. Gradually blend in the milk, bring to the boil, cook until smooth and thickened, add seasoning and grated cheese. Serve the dumplings hot with the sauce.

Jam suet pudding

Cooking time: 1½ hours
Preparation time: 15 minutes
Main cooking utensils: 1½-pint (¾-litre) pudding basin, steamer,
saucepan, foil or greaseproof paper.
Serves: 4

Imperial	Metric
4 oz. flour (with plain flour use 1 teaspoon baking powder)	100 g. flour (with plain flour use 1 teaspoon baking powder)
pinch salt	pinch salt
2 oz. sugar	50 g. sugar
2 oz. shredded suet	50 g. shredded suet
about 2 tablespoons milk	about 2 tablespoons milk
2 tablespoons jam	2 tablespoons jam

1. Sieve the flour or flour and baking powder with the salt; add the sugar and the shredded suet.
2. Gradually stir in the milk, binding the mixture together. This should be a stiff consistency but as flour varies, you may need a little extra milk.
3. Put the jam at the bottom of the greased basin and put the mixture on top.
4. Cover with greased foil or greased greaseproof paper.
5. Steam over boiling water.
6. When cooked, turn out on to a hot dish. Heat more jam as a sauce.

Variation
Use 2 oz. (50 g.) flour and 2 oz. (50 g.) breadcrumbs.

Orange pudding : Add the grated rind of an orange to the mixture. Mix with orange juice instead of milk. Put marmalade at the bottom of the basin.

Golden cap pudding

Cooking time: 1½ hours
Preparation time: 20 minutes
Main cooking utensils: 1½-pint (¾-litre) basin, steamer, saucepan,
  foil or greaseproof paper
Serves: 4

Imperial	Metric
4 oz. margarine or butter	100 g. margarine or butter
4 oz. castor sugar	100 g. castor sugar
2 eggs	2 eggs
4 oz. self-raising flour (or plain flour and 1 level teaspoon baking powder)	100 g. self-raising flour (or plain flour and 1 level teaspoon baking powder)
2–3 tablespoons golden syrup	2–3 tablespoons golden syrup

1. Cream together the margarine or butter and sugar until soft and light.

2. Gradually beat in the eggs, adding a little sieved flour if the mixture looks like curdling.

3. Fold in the remainder of the flour; if the eggs are small add 1 tablespoon water.

4. Put golden syrup into the bottom of the greased basin.

5. Cover with the pudding mixture, allowing enough room for the pudding to rise well.

6. Cover with greased paper or foil.

7. Steam over boiling water.

8. Turn out and top with more hot golden syrup.

Variations

Black top pudding: Use blackcurrant jam instead of syrup.

Red cap pudding: Use red jam instead of syrup. Flavour the sponge mixture with spice, chocolate, etc. For a more economical pudding use 2 oz. (50 g.) margarine, 2 oz. (50 g.) sugar, and 1 egg with the flour. Mix with milk or water to a soft dropping consistency.

Spiced apple charlotte

Cooking time: 1 hour
Preparation time: 20 minutes
Main cooking utensils: 2-pint (1-litre) pie dish, saucepan
Oven temperature: very moderate (350°F., 180°C., Gas Mark 4)
Oven position: centre
Serves: 4–6

Imperial

Crumb mixture:
6 oz. fine white breadcrumbs
4 oz. chopped suet
2 oz. granulated or brown sugar
Fruit mixture:
1 oz. butter
2 tablespoons water
1½ lb. cooking apples
2 oz. brown sugar
1 oz. sultanas or seedless raisins
¼ level teaspoon cinnamon or
  spice
Topping:
1 oz. brown sugar
1 oz. butter

Metric

Crumb mixture:
150 g. fine white breadcrumbs
100 g. chopped suet
50 g. granulated or brown sugar
Fruit mixture:
25 g. butter
2 tablespoons water
¾ kg. cooking apples
50 g. brown sugar
25 g. sultanas or seedless raisins
¼ level teaspoon cinnamon or
  spice
Topping:
25 g. brown sugar
25 g. butter

1. Mix the breadcrumbs, suet and granulated or brown sugar well together.
2. Press three-quarters on to the bottom and sides of the pie dish.
3. Melt the butter in a pan, add the water, the peeled cored and diced apples and the brown sugar.
4. Cover and heat gently, shaking the stirring occasionally, till the apples are well glazed but not too soft.
5. Remove from the heat, stir in the sultanas and cinnamon.
6. Pour into the prepared pie dish and top with remaining crumb mixture, pressing down neatly.
7. Wipe the edge of the dish, sprinkle crumbs with layer of brown sugar, dot with butter.
8. Bake in the centre of the oven until golden brown. Serve hot with cream or custard.

Variation
Use the same recipe with halved plums.

Fruit crumble

Cooking time: 30–40 minutes plus time to cook fruit
Preparation time: few minutes plus time to prepare fruit
Main cooking utensils: saucepan for firmer fruit, pie or ovenproof dish
Oven temperature: moderate (350–375°F., 180–190°C., Gas Mark 4–5)
Oven position: centre or just above centre
Serves: 4

Imperial	Metric
1 lb. prepared fruit	$\frac{1}{2}$ kg. prepared fruit
sugar to taste	sugar to taste
little water with firm fruit	little water with firm fruit
Crumble:	*Crumble:*
2 oz. margarine or butter	50 g. margarine or butter
4 oz. flour, plain or self-raising	100 g. flour, plain or self-raising
3–4 oz. sugar	75–100 g. sugar

1. Prepare the fruit, slicing apples, dicing rhubarb, halving and stoning plums and washing soft fruits.

2. With firm fruits, simmer until nearly tender with sugar to taste and a little water. The mixture must be fairly firm. With soft fruits, there is no need to pre-cook or soften.

3. Put the fruit into the dish.

4. Rub the margarine or butter into the flour, add the sugar and sprinkle over the top of the fruit; press down firmly.

5. Bake until crisp and golden brown. Serve hot, with cream or custard.

Variation

Mix dried fruits with the fresh fruit; add a little spice to the flour or use 1 oz. (25 g.) coconut instead of 1 oz. (25 g.) flour.

Golden apricot pudding

Cooking time: 1 hour
Preparation time: 20 minutes
Main cooking utensils: saucepan, 2-pint (1-litre) ovenproof dish
Oven temperature: moderate (350–375°F., 180–190°C., Gas Mark 4–5)
Oven position: centre
Serves: 4–6

Imperial	Metric
1 lb. fresh apricots	400 g. fresh apricots
¼ pint water	125 ml. water
4 oz. soft brown sugar	100 g. soft brown sugar
Topping:	*Topping:*
3 oz. butter	75 g. butter
3 oz. sugar	75 g. sugar
4 oz. self-raising flour or plain flour and 1 level teaspoon baking powder	100 g. self-raising flour or plain flour and 1 level teaspoon baking powder
4 tablespoons milk	4 tablespoons milk
3 egg whites	3 egg whites
½ oz. flaked or chopped nuts	15 g. flaked or chopped nuts
Golden sauce:	*Golden sauce:*
3 egg yolks	3 egg yolks
1 oz. castor sugar	25 g. castor sugar
3 tablespoons apricot juice	3 tablespoons apricot juice
1 teaspoon lemon juice	1 teaspoon lemon juice

1. Halve and stone the apricots, cook in water with sugar until just tender.
2. Drain fruit, reserving the syrup.
3. Put fruit into the well greased dish.
4. Prepare topping by creaming butter and sugar together until light and fluffy.
5. Fold in the sieved flour and the milk.
6. Whisk egg whites and gently fold into the creamed mixture.
7. Spread over fruit, sprinkle with flaked nuts and bake until firm to touch.
8. 10 minutes before serving, blend egg yolks and sugar together and slowly stir in apricot juice and lemon juice in a basin over simmering water.
9. Whisk until light and foamy. Serve hot with cream or sauce.

Variation

Use any other fruit — plums or rhubarb are particularly suitable.

Chocolate casserole pudding

Cooking time: 45 minutes
Preparation time: 15 minutes
Main cooking utensils: shallow casserole, tin for water
Oven temperature: very moderate to moderate (350–375°F.,
    180–190°C., Gas Mark 4–5)
Oven position: centre
Serves: 4–5

Imperial	Metric
3 oz. margarine	75 g. margarine
3 oz. sugar	75 g. sugar
3 eggs	3 eggs
3 oz. flour (with plain flour use 1 level teaspoon baking powder)	75 g. flour (with plain flour use 1 level teaspoon baking powder)
1 oz. cocoa	25 g. cocoa
good ½ pint milk	275 ml. milk
To decorate:	*To decorate:*
little castor sugar	little castor sugar

1. Cream the margarine and sugar until soft and light.
2. Gradually beat in the egg yolks, then fold in the sieved flour, cocoa and the milk. You may find the mixture curdles but this is quite in order.
3. Lastly fold in the stiffly beaten egg whites.
4. Put into the greased casserole and stand in a tin of water.
5. This pudding will separate during cooking and give you a very light fluffy texture on top with a more moist saucelike texture underneath.
6. If you want a slightly crisp topping, do not cover the casserole. If you wish the topping to be soft, put a lid or foil on the casserole.
7. Bake for the time and at temperature given.
8. Sprinkle the top with sugar and serve hot or cold with cream or custard.

Variation

Use coffee in place of milk or omit cocoa and use the grated rind of 2 lemons and juice of 2 lemons and enough milk to give 13 tablespoons.

Fruit suet pudding

Cooking time: 2 hours
Preparation time: 15 minutes
Main cooking utensils: pudding basin, steamer, saucepan,
   greaseproof paper or foil
Serves: 4

Imperial

Suet crust pastry:
8 oz. self-raising flour or plain
    flour and 2 level teaspoons
    baking powder
pinch salt
4 oz. shredded suet
cold water to mix
Filling:
1 lb. prepared fruit
2–3 tablespoons sugar
little water

Metric

Suet crust pastry:
200 g. self-raising flour or plain
    flour and 2 level teaspoons
    powder
pinch salt
100 g. shredded suet
cold water to mix
Filling:
½ kg. prepared fruit
2–3 tablespoons sugar
little water

1. Sieve the flour and salt, add the suet and bind with water.
2. Roll out and use two-thirds to line the pudding basin.
3. Put the prepared fruit into the lined basin with sugar and water if necessary.
4. Cover the remainder of the pastry, seal edges firmly.
5. Cover with greased foil and steam over boiling water for 2 hours.
6. Turn out carefully and serve with hot custard sauce.

Variation

Use different types of fruit. If using hard fruit you need 2–3 tablespoons water; 1 tablespoon water with fruit that softens and makes a little juice (like blackcurrants); no water with fruit like rhubarb that makes a lot of juice. A mixture of fruits can also be used, as in the picture.

Blackberry roly poly

Cooking time: 40–45 minutes
Preparation time: 20 minutes
Main cooking utensil: ovenproof dish
Oven temperature: hot (425–450°F., 220–230°C., Gas Mark 7–8),
    then moderate (375°F., 190°C., Gas Mark 5)
Oven position: centre
Serves: 4–6

Imperial	Metric
8 oz. self-raising flour	200 g. self-raising flour
pinch salt	pinch salt
3 oz. butter	75 g. butter
1 oz. castor sugar	25 g. castor sugar
2 level teaspoons finely grated lemon rind	2 level teaspoons finely grated lemon rind
about 4 tablespoons milk to mix	about 4 tablespoons milk to mix
Filling:	*Filling:*
12 oz. fresh blackberries	300 g. fresh blackberries
little water	little water
2–3 oz. castor sugar	50–75 g. castor sugar
3 tablespoons water	3 tablespoons water
Topping:	*Topping:*
1 egg or milk	1 egg or milk
2 level teaspoons castor sugar	2 level teaspoons castor sugar
1 oz. butter	25 g. butter

1. Sieve the flour and salt together.
2. Rub in the butter and add sugar and lemon rind.
3. Mix to a soft dough with the milk, roll out into a rectangle approximately 12 inches by 10 inches (30 cm. by 25 cm.).
4. Cover with 10 oz. (250 g.) of the fruit, to within 1 inch (2½ cm.) of the edge.
5. Moisten the edges of the dough with water, sprinkle the fruit with sugar, then roll up like a Swiss roll.
6. Press joins carefully together to seal then lift into the dish.
7. Make three slits on the top of the roll, brush with beaten egg or milk, sprinkle with castor sugar and dot with butter.
8. Pour 3 tablespoons water into the dish.
9. Bake in a hot oven for 15 minutes then add the rest of the blackberries on top of the slits and reduce heat to moderate for the rest of the time. Serve with cream or custard.

Variation

Use 2 oz. (50 g.) butter only and a little extra milk.

Treacle tart

Cooking time: 25–30 minutes
Preparation time: 20 minutes
Main cooking utensil: 9-inch (23-cm.) ovenproof plate
Oven temperature: moderately hot to hot (400–425°F., 200–220°C., Gas Mark 6–7)
Oven position: centre
Serves: 4–6

Imperial	Metric
Shortcrust pastry:	*Shortcrust pastry:*
8 oz. flour, self-raising or plain	200 g. flour, self-raising or plain
pinch salt	pinch salt
2 oz. margarine	50 g. margarine
2 oz. lard	50 g. lard
about 2 tablespoons cold water	about 2 tablespoons cold water
Filling:	*Filling:*
4 tablespoons soft fine	4 tablespoons soft fine
breadcrumbs	breadcrumbs
4 tablespoons warmed golden	4 tablespoons warmed golden
syrup	syrup
juice of 1 lemon	juice of 1 lemon

1. Sieve the flour and salt, rub in the fat until it resembles fine breadcrumbs.

2. Add enough water to make a firm dough.

3. Roll out on a floured board, line the plate, trim and decorate the edges, see below.

4. Prick base with fork.

5. Mix breadcrumbs, syrup and lemon juice. Spread over pastry.

6. Re-roll pastry trimmings, cut narrow strips. Twist them over filling, damping ends so they stick in position.

7. Bake for time and at temperature given; lower heat after 20 minutes if necessary. Serve hot or cold with custard or cream.

Note: To ensure a crisp base to tarts, etc., stand pie plate on baking sheet, heated in oven, or bake pastry blind in a hot oven (425–450°F., 220–230°C., Gas Mark 7–8) for 10 minutes, remove paper and baking beans, add warm filling and complete cooking for 20 minutes in a moderate oven (375°F., 190°C., Gas Mark 4–5). To decorate pastry, either flute by pinching edges with finger and thumb, or press the edges with the prongs of a fork.

Variation
Use cornflakes instead of breadcrumbs.

Blackberry and apple dumplings

Cooking time: 40 minutes
Preparation time: 30 minutes
Main cooking utensil: baking sheet
Oven temperature: moderately hot (375–400°F., 190–200°C., Gas
   Mark 5–6)
Oven position: centre
Serves: 4

Imperial

Shortcrust pastry:
6 oz. margarine
12 oz. plain flour
pinch salt
3½–4 tablespoons water
Filling:
4 medium-sized cooking apples
4 oz. blackberries
2 oz. castor sugar

Metric

Shortcrust pastry:
150 g. margarine
300 g. plain flour
pinch salt
3½–4 tablespoons water
Filling:
4 medium-sized cooking apples
100 g. blackberries
50 g. castor sugar

1. Rub the margarine into the flour, sieved with a pinch of salt, until it resembles fine breadcrumbs, mix with water to form a firm dough, divide into five.
2. Roll four of the portions into rounds large enough to cover the apples completely; roll out remaining portion and use to make leaves and stems.
3. Peel and core apples, place each in the centre of a round of pastry.
4. Fill with blackberries and sugar.
5. Damp the edges of the pastry, draw up to cover the apples, press together to seal.
6. Turn apples over, put on baking sheet.
7. Damp the backs of leaves and stems with water, press on top of the apples.
8. Bake until golden brown. Sprinkle with sugar and serve hot or cold with custard or cream.

Note : Make the pastry a little softer than for a pie or tart so that it wraps round the apples without tearing or breaking.

Variation

Fill apples with brown sugar and sultanas, or bramble jelly, or with mincemeat. Use pears instead of apples.

Pancakes

Cooking time: 10–15 minutes
Preparation time: 10 minutes
Main cooking utensils: frying pan, saucepan
Serves: 4–6

Imperial	**Metric**
Pancake batter:	*Pancake batter:*
4 oz. flour	110 g. flour
pinch salt	pinch salt
2 eggs	2 eggs
just under $\frac{1}{2}$ pint milk	275 ml. milk
For frying:	*For frying:*
little butter or oil	little butter or oil
Traditional topping:	*Traditional topping:*
sugar	sugar
lemon	lemon
Fruit filling and topping:	*Fruit filling and topping:*
1 lb. peeled cooking apples	$\frac{1}{2}$ kg. peeled cooking apples
3 tablespoons water	3 tablespoons water
2 oz. sugar	50 g. sugar
3 tablespoons apricot jam	3 tablespoons apricot jam
few raisins or sultanas	few raisins or sultanas

1. Sieve together the flour and salt.
2. Add the beaten eggs and mix well.
3. Add the milk and beat again.
4. Melt enough butter or oil in a small frying pan just to cover the base.
5. Pour in enough batter to make a thin pancake.
6. Cook on either side until brown.
7. If serving the traditional way, tip on to sugared paper, roll, and serve on a hot dish with wedges of lemon. The pancakes can be kept until ready to serve on an uncovered hot plate over hot water or in the oven.
8. If serving with a fruit topping, simmer the apples with the water and sugar until tender, blend with the apricot jam and raisins. Use half as a filling for the pancakes, roll or fold, then top with the remainder.

Note : Pancakes, though they are traditionally served on a Shrove Tuesday, can be served with various fillings throughout the year.
The exact metric conversions given above give a better result.

Pineapple fritters

Cooking time: 10 minutes
Preparation time: 10 minutes
Main cooking utensils: deep fat pan and frying basket
Serves: 4

Imperial	**Metric**
1 medium-sized can pineapple rings	1 medium-sized can pineapple rings
½ oz. flour	15 g. flour
lard for frying	lard for frying
little castor sugar	little castor sugar
Fritter batter:	*Fritter batter:*
4 oz. flour	100 g. flour
pinch salt	pinch salt
1 egg	1 egg
¼ pint milk	125 ml. milk
2 tablespoons water	2 tablespoons water

1. To make the batter, sieve the flour and salt into a basin, add the egg, beat well, then gradually beat in the milk and the water to give a thick coating consistency.

2. Drain the pineapple rings and dust lightly with flour.

3. Heat the lard until a cube of bread turns golden brown within a minute.

4. Dip the pineapple rings into the batter and fry in the hot lard until crisp and golden brown.

5. Drain on crumpled tissue paper.

6. Dust with castor sugar before serving hot, either with the syrup from the can or with sauce. A raspberry or strawberry jam sauce goes well with pineapple.

Variation

Use rings of apple (cook more slowly to ensure they are soft), bananas and other fruits.

Bread and butter pudding

Cooking time: 45 minutes
Preparation time: 15 minutes
Main cooking utensil: 2-pint (1-litre) pie dish
Oven temperature: very moderate (325–350°F., 170–180°C., Gas
    Mark 3–4)
Oven position: centre
Serves: 4

Imperial	**Metric**
3 slices bread and butter	3 slices bread and butter
2–3 oz. dried fruit	50–75 g. dried fruit
2 eggs	2 eggs
1–1½ oz. sugar	25–40 g. sugar
¾ pint milk	425 ml. milk

1. Cut the bread and butter into triangles.
2. Put into the pie dish and add dried fruit.
3. Beat the eggs with the sugar, pour on the warmed milk, then strain over the bread and butter.
4. Bake until just firm and set. Move the pudding towards the top of the oven before serving to encourage the bread and butter to brown and crisp slightly. If baking in a fairly deep dish it will take longer. Serve hot.

Note : This pudding improves if allowed to stand for a short time before it is cooked.

Variation
Make a richer pudding by adding 2 oz. (50 g.) crystallised peel and 4 oz. (100 g.) dried fruit. Top with grated nutmeg before cooking.

Fruit cobbler

Cooking time: 25 minutes
Preparation time: 10 minutes
Main cooking utensils: wide shallow ovenproof dish or pie dish
Oven temperature: hot (425–450°F., 220–230°C., Gas Mark 7–8)
Oven position: coolest part then towards top
Serves: 4

Imperial
1 can pie filling or fresh fruit
Cobbler:
4 oz. self-raising flour or plain
   flour with 2 level teaspoons
   baking powder
1 oz. margarine
1 oz. sugar
milk to mix

Metric
1 can pie filling or fresh fruit
Cobbler:
100 g. self-raising flour or plain
   flour with 2 level teaspoons
   baking powder
25 g. margarine
25 g. sugar
milk to mix

1. Tip the pie filling into the pie dish and heat for approximately 10 minutes in the oven.
2. Sieve the flour into a basin, rub in margarine until it is the consistency of breadcrumbs, add the sugar and enough milk to make a soft rolling consistency.
3. Roll out to about $\frac{1}{4}$-inch ($\frac{1}{2}$-cm.) thickness.
4. Cut into small rounds and arrange round the edge of the hot pie filling.
5. Bake for nearly 15 minutes towards the top of the oven until golden brown.

Note: When the cobbler (scone mixture) is brown the oven may be reduced to very low in order to keep the pudding hot without burning it.

Variation
Any fruit may be used in this way which makes a very pleasant change from pastry.

Egg custard

Cooking time: 1½–2 hours
Preparation time: few minutes
Main cooking utensils: to bake, 1½-pint (¾-litre) pie dish, tin for water; to steam, basin or soufflé dish, steamer, saucepan, foil or greaseproof paper; to boil, double saucepan
Oven temperature: slow to very moderate (300–325°F., 150–170°C., Gas Mark 2–3)
Oven position: coolest part
Serves: 4

Imperial	**Metric**
For a lightly set custard:	*For a lightly set custard:*
2 eggs or egg yolks	2 eggs or egg yolks
1 oz. sugar	25 g. sugar
1 pint milk	550 ml. milk
little grated nutmeg	little grated nutmeg
For a firmer custard:	*For a firmer custard:*
3–4 eggs or egg yolks	3–4 eggs or egg yolks
1 oz. sugar	25 g. sugar
1 pint milk	550 ml. milk

1. Whisk the eggs and sugar lightly.

2. Warm the milk if wished — this hastens cooking slightly. Do not boil.

3. Pour the milk over the eggs and strain into the dish (this makes sure no particles of egg remain on top).

4. To bake the pudding, stand dish in the tin of water — this helps to prevent the custard drying or curdling. Top with grated nutmeg; there is no need to cover with paper or foil. Cook until just set.

5. To steam, strain custard into a dish, cover with foil or greased paper. Stand in a steamer and cook over hot but not boiling water until just set. (You should always be able to bear your fingers in the water.)

6. To boil, cook in the top of the double saucepan or basin over hot but not boiling water until thick enough to coat the back of a wooden spoon. The custard should never boil, but must cook very slowly to prevent curdling.

Gooseberry layer shortcake

Cooking time: 25–30 minutes
Preparation time: 25 minutes
Main cooking utensil: 7-inch (18-cm.) cake tin
Oven temperature: moderately hot (400°F., 200°C., Gas Mark 6)
Oven position: centre
Serves: 4

Imperial	Metric
Filling:	*Filling:*
1 lb. fresh gooseberries	$\frac{1}{2}$ kg. fresh gooseberries
3 oz. castor sugar	75 g. castor sugar
2 tablespoons water	2 tablespoons water
Shortcake pastry:	*Shortcake pastry:*
3 oz. butter	75 g. butter
6 oz. self-raising flour or plain flour with 1$\frac{1}{2}$ level teaspoons baking powder	150 g. self-raising flour or plain flour with 1$\frac{1}{2}$ level teaspoons baking powder
3 oz. castor	75 g. castor sugar
$\frac{1}{2}$ level teaspoon ground nutmeg	$\frac{1}{2}$ level teaspoon ground nutmeg
Topping:	*Topping:*
little extra sugar	little extra sugar
cream	cream

1. Top and tail the gooseberries.
2. Dissolve the sugar in the water, add the fruit and stir over a low heat for 5 minutes. Cool, drain fruit if there is any juice.
3. Rub fat into flour until the mixture resembles breadcrumbs.
4. Add sugar and nutmeg.
5. Press half of the mixture into the greased cake tin.
6. Spread fruit over the top and sprinkle with the remaining rubbed-in mixture.
7. Bake for time and at temperature given. Turn out of the tin.
8. Sprinkle with castor or sieved icing sugar and serve hot or cold with fresh cream.

Note: The mixture is very crumbly and fragile. To make it easier to handle bind with an egg and very little milk.

Variation

This shortcake mixture may be baked in two 6- to 7-inch (15- to 18-cm.) tins for approximately 20 minutes and sandwiched with fruit and cream.

Lemon meringue pie

Cooking time: pastry, 20–25 minutes; filling, 15 minutes; meringue, 30–40 minutes
Preparation time: 35 minutes
Main cooking utensils: 7- to 8-inch (18- to 20-cm.) deep flan ring or tin, saucepan
Oven temperature: pastry, moderately hot (425°F., 220°C., Gas Mark 7); meringue, slow (300°F., 150°C., Gas Mark 2) or see variation
Oven position: centre
Serves: 5–6

Imperial

6 oz. shortcrust pastry (see page 105) or sweet rich shortcrust pastry (see page 123)

Filling:
2 oz. castor sugar
pinch salt
1 oz. cornflour
small can evaporated milk
¼ pint boiling water
2 eggs
juice of 1 lemon
grated rind of 1 lemon

Meringue:
2–4 oz. castor sugar

Metric

150 g. shortcrust pastry (see page 105) or sweet rich shortcrust pastry (see page 123)

Filling:
50 g. castor sugar
pinch salt
25 g. cornflour
small can evaporated milk
125 ml. boiling water
2 eggs
juice of 1 lemon
grated rind of 1 lemon

Meringue:
50–100 g. castor sugar

1. Roll out the pastry, line a flan ring or tin, and bake 'blind' until brown.

2. Mix sugar, salt and cornflour, blend with the milk, gradually stir in the boiling water.

3. Bring to the boil over a gentle heat and simmer for 5 minutes.

4. Separate yolks from whites of eggs.

5. Remove mixture from heat, add the beaten egg yolks and cook for a further 2–3 minutes over gentle heat, stirring; do not boil.

6. Add lemon juice and rind.

7. Allow to cool, pour into the prepared pastry case.

8. Whisk egg whites until stiff.

9. Gradually whisk in half the sugar, then fold in the rest of the sugar.

10. Pile or pipe meringue on top of pie, bake in the centre of a slow oven for time given.

Variation

To serve cold set the meringue for 1–1¼ hours in a very cool oven (275°F., 140°C., Gas Mark 1). Use 4 oz. (100 g.) sugar.

Honeycomb mould

Cooking time: 10–15 minutes
Preparation time: 15 minutes
Main cooking utensils: double saucepan, 2-pint (1-litre) fancy mould
Serves: 4–6

Imperial	Metric
1 packet lime or lemon flavoured jelly	1 packet lime or lemon flavoured jelly
½ pint boiling water	275 ml. boiling water
2 eggs	2 eggs
¼ pint milk	150 ml. milk
grated lemon or lime rind (optional)	grated lemon or lime rind (optional)
3 oz. castor sugar	75 g. castor sugar

1. Make up jelly as directed on the packet but use ½ pint (275 ml.) boiling water only.

2. Separate the egg yolks and whites.

3. Heat the milk and yolks in the top of a double saucepan, cook until the mixture thickens and thinly coats the back of a wooden spoon. Add a little rind of lemon or lime, if wished.

4. Stir in 2 oz. (50 g.) of the sugar and the liquid jelly, then cool.

5. Whisk the egg whites very stiffly, gradually beat in the sugar, then fold this into the cold but not set jelly mixture.

6. Stir quickly, then pour into the rinsed mould.

7. Chill until firmly set, then turn out on to a dish.

Variation

If the egg whites and sugar at stage 5 are folded into the half-set jelly, you turn this into a simple mousse. If you like, serve the mould on a bed of extra jelly, chopped up.

Orange cheese cake

Cooking time: 45 minutes
Preparation time: 25–30 minutes
Main cooking utensils: 8-inch (20-cm.) flan ring, baking tray
Oven temperature: hot (425–450°F., 220–230°C., Gas Mark 7–8),
    then moderate (325–350°F., 170–180°C., Gas Mark 3–4)
Oven position: centre
Serves: 6–8

Imperial	Metric
Sweet rich shortcrust:	*Sweet rich shortcrust:*
8 oz. plain flour	200 g. plain flour
pinch salt	pinch salt
5 oz. butter	125 g. butter
2 oz. castor sugar	50 g. castor sugar
1 egg yolk	1 egg yolk
about 1½ teaspoons water	about 1½ teaspoons water
Filling:	*Filling:*
8 oz. cottage cheese	200 g. cottage cheese
1 egg	1 egg
1 egg white	1 egg white
1 oz. cornflour	25 g. cornflour
3 oz. castor sugar	75 g. castor sugar
rind of 1 orange	rind of 1 orange
juice of 1 orange	juice of 1 orange
4 oz. thick cream	100 ml. thick cream

1. Sieve the flour and salt. Rub in the butter until the mixture resembles breadcrumbs.
2. Add the sugar and bind with the egg yolk and water. Chill if necessary.
3. Roll out three-quarters of the pastry and line the flan ring. Reserve the rest of the pastry.
4. Sieve the cottage cheese.
5. Blend the egg and egg white with the cornflour.
6. Add the rest of the filling ingredients and mix well.
7. Turn the mixture into the flan case.
8. Bake in a hot oven for 10 minutes until the filling begins to set.
9. Remove from the oven and arrange the lattice of pastry on top of the flan.
10. Return to the oven and bake for a further 35 minutes in a very moderate oven until a pale golden brown.

Variation
Use lemon juice and lemon rind in place of orange.

Scotch pancakes

Cooking time: 4 minutes each batch
Preparation time: 10 minutes
Main cooking utensil: griddle or thick frying pan
Makes: 8–12 pancakes

Imperial	Metric
4 oz. flour (with plain flour use either 2 teaspoons baking powder or ½ small teaspoon bicarbonate of soda and 1 small teaspoon cream of tartar)	100 g. flour (with plain flour use either 2 teaspoons baking powder or ½ small teaspoon bicarbonate of soda and 1 small teaspoon cream of tartar)
pinch salt	pinch salt
1 oz. sugar	25 g. sugar
1 egg	1 egg
¼ pint milk	125 ml. milk
1 oz. melted margarine (optional)	25 g. melted margarine (optional)

1. Sieve together the dry ingredients.
2. Beat in first the egg, then the milk.
3. Lastly stir in the melted margarine. This is not essential but it does help to keep the scones moist.
4. Grease and warm the griddle, hot plate or frying pan. It is best to use the bottom of the frying pan — the part that usually goes over the heat.
5. To test if the heat is correct, drop a teaspoon of the mixture on the heated surface, and if it goes golden brown within 1 minute, the plate is ready.
6. Drop spoonfuls of the mixture on to the plate.
7. Cook for about 2 minutes, then turn and cook for a further 2 minutes.
8. To test if cooked, press firmly with the back of a knife, and if no batter comes from the sides and the scones feel firm lift out and cool on a wire sieve. Serve with butter, butter and jam or as illustrated, topped with butter and served with a thick apple purée.

Note: The scones are better made with plain flour and 2 teaspoons baking powder since this is a higher percentage of raising agent.

Wholemeal nut bread

Cooking time: 1¼–1½ hours
Preparation time: 15 minutes
Main cooking utensil: 2-lb. (1-kg.) loaf tin
Oven temperature: moderate (375°F., 190°C., Gas Mark 5)
Oven position: centre
Serves: 10–12

Imperial	**Metric**
1 lb. wholemeal flour	400 g. wholemeal flour
2 level teaspoons baking powder	2 level teaspoons baking powder
$\frac{1}{2}$ teaspoon salt	$\frac{1}{2}$ teaspoon salt
2 eggs	2 eggs
$\frac{1}{2}$ pint milk	250 ml. milk
2 oz. melted butter	50 g. melted butter
4 oz. chopped walnuts	100 g. chopped walnuts

1. Mix together the flour, baking powder and salt.
2. Lightly beat the eggs and add to the dry ingredients with the milk and melted butter.
3. Mix to a smooth soft dough.
4. Add the chopped walnuts.
5. Turn into a well-greased loaf tin.
6. Bake for the time and at temperature given until firm to the touch. Serve with butter, cheese, and tomatoes.

Note: If making wholemeal bread for the first time, be prepared for it to take longer in cooking than white bread since it absorbs more moisture. It is therefore advisable to use a slightly lower oven temperature. Wholemeal bread takes longer to toast, therefore if using an automatic toaster remember it should be re-set when toasting wholemeal bread after white bread.

Variations
Divide the dough in two and bake in two 1-lb. loaf tins for 1 hour. For extra flavour, celery salt may be used in place of ordinary salt.

Acknowledgements

The following photographs are by courtesy of:

Beechams Foods Limited: page 112
Cadbury Schweppes Foods Limited: pages 82, 96, 110
Danish Agricultural Council: page 72
Farrows Rice: pages 10, 20
Fruit Producers' Council: pages 104, 124
Libby McNeill and Libby Limited: pages 40, 42
George Newnes Limited: page 88
New Zealand Lamb Information Bureau: page 32
Potato Marketing Board: pages 74, 78
RHM Foods Limited: pages 26, 28, 34, 58, 86, 98, 102
Van den Berghs Limited: page 36
White Fish Authority: pages 8, 18